RICH WORLD, POOR WORLD

Melanie Jarman

Smart Apple Media

First published in 2006 by Franklin Watts
338 Euston Road, London NW1 3BH

Franklin Watts Australia, Hachette Children's Books
Level 17/207 Kent Street, Sydney NSW 2000

Series editor: Sarah Peutrill, **Art director:** Jonathan Hair, **Design:** Proof Books, **Additional research:** Camille Warren, **Picture researcher:** Sophie Hartley

Picture and text credits: see page 48.

Note on Web sites:
Every effort has been made by the publishers to ensure that the Web sites in this book contain no inappropriate or offensive material. However, because of the nature of the Internet, it is impossible to guarantee that the contents of these sites will not be altered. We strongly advise that Internet access be supervised by a responsible adult.

Published in the United States by Smart Apple Media
2140 Howard Drive West, North Mankato, Minnesota 56003

Library of Congress Cataloging-in-Publication Data

Jarman, Melanie.
Rich world, poor world / by Melanie Jarman.
p. cm. — (What's your view?)
Includes index.
ISBN-13 : 978-1-58340-973-2
1. Poverty—Developing countries. 2. Developing countries—Economic conditions. I. Title. II. Series.

HC59.72.P6J37 2006
339.4'6091724—dc22 2005037709

9 8 7 6 5 4 3 2 1

Contents

What's the issue?

A DIFFERENT WORLD

A child wakes and stretches her arms. She spreads wide the fingers on each hand. The skin on her hands is rough and blotchy. Is it the water she has been drinking? One in 5 children in the world has no access to safe water: 6 children in a classroom of 30. Is it a sign of HIV? Many of her friends have suffered from that illness. The child brings her hands to rest on her stomach. Here is a familiar pain: the pain of meals missed. Not just today's breakfast, but yesterday's, and last week's, and last month's.

The child does not know it, for her hands never held a schoolbook (her family could never afford to send her to school), but she is not alone. The levels of wealth that many people experience in developed countries are just not normal for many people in the world. Of the world's 2.2 billion children, almost half—about 1 billion—are living in poverty.

A GROWING PROBLEM

Our world is so wealthy that global income is more than $30 trillion a year. In richer parts of the world, the average income is more than $40,000 a year. But 40 percent of our world's population lives on less than $2.10 a day and has problems getting safe water, decent food, and basic healthcare. Though an increasingly globalized economy sometimes makes our world seem smaller, the gulf between rich and poor is huge, and it is growing. This is the case both between different countries and within individual countries.

WHAT'S BEING DONE?

The international community has said it will do something about global poverty. In the year 2000, the United Nations launched a set of Millennium Development Goals (see page 43) aimed at making a real difference by the year 2015. If the world fails to meet these goals, 45 million more children will die between now and 2015.

While there is wide agreement over the need to tackle poverty, there is much debate on how to go about it. This book introduces some of these debates. Each one gives you the opinions of several people or organizations, plus relevant statistics as a starting point. "Conflicting Evidence" explores how research may seem to support either side. Each spread concludes with some Web sites to help you investigate the debate further and begin to decide which side of the debate you agree with. If you wish to hold a debate on one or more of these issues, check out the debating tips on page 46.

NOTE ON QUOTES

Quotes presented in this book in a specific context should not be understood to commit their source to one side of that debate. They are simply illustrations of the possible viewpoints in each debate.

A slum in Mumbai (Bombay), India, sits in stark contrast with the rich suburb of Bandra behind it. Financial inequality exists within countries as well as between them.

Q: Are developed countries to blame for the debt crisis?

THE INTERNATIONAL debt crisis is a big problem for developing countries. In the 1960s and 1970s, many developing countries borrowed from banks and institutions in developed countries. In the years since the money was first borrowed, interest owed on the original amount has added up, and the debt has grown considerably. Finding out how the situation came about is an important step in resolving it.

"...AND SO IT HAS BEEN AGREED THAT WE BRING THE INTERNATIONAL DEBT CRISIS TO AN END AS SOON AS WE HAVE FOUND AN ALTERNATIVE WAY OF KEEPING THE DEVELOPING NATIONS POOR.

Developed countries, and organizations such as the World Bank, have been accused of not doing enough to end the debt crisis.

YES "While the international financial institutions claim they cannot 'afford' to write off the debts owed them, it is the case that the IMF has gold reserves totaling more than $30 billion and that the International Bank for Reconstruction and Development alone had a net income of more than $5 billion in 2003."

The 50 Years is Enough Network

CASE STUDY 1

ZAIRE
Much of the debt owed by developing countries today is the result of loans made to military dictators as part of the struggle for international influence during the Cold War (1945–90).

Mobutu Sese Seko, the ruler of Zaire (now the Democratic Republic of Congo) between 1965 and 1997, was a corrupt leader. Yet the West considered him to be on its side during the Cold War. The International Monetary Fund (IMF) awarded Mobutu's government one of the largest loans ever made to an African country. While commercial banks refused to lend to Mobutu, Western governments lent him nearly $3 billion.

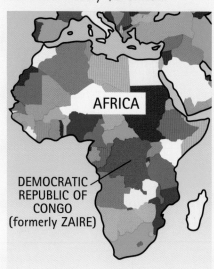

AFRICA

DEMOCRATIC REPUBLIC OF CONGO (formerly ZAIRE)

CASE STUDY 2

LOAN PUSHING?

In the early 1970s, European banks found that people in developed countries were not borrowing as much as the banks wanted them to. This was a problem, as banks need to lend money out in order to earn interest and accumulate more money. Faced with too much money and not enough borrowers, the banks encouraged developing countries to sign up for loans. Interest rates were low, so many countries took advantage of these offers. However, over time, the interest rate on loans increased—and the overall debt rose with it.

✹ STATISTICALLY SPEAKING

• The 42 most heavily indebted countries in the world currently owe about one and a half times their annual income to richer countries.
• Between 1980 and 1996, countries in sub-Saharan Africa paid twice the sum of their total debt as interest, but they still owed three times more in 1996 than they did in 1980.

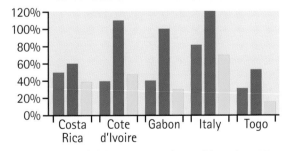

A worldwide slowdown in growth between 1975 and 1994 contributed to the debt crisis

■ actual debt to country's wealth ratio, 1975
■ actual debt to country's wealth ratio, 1994
▢ ratio as it would have been if growth had not slowed down

NO

"Many poor countries had borrowed [in the 1970s and '80s] to fund domestic projects on the back of the commodity price boom, believing that the high prices and export earnings would be sustained. But the oil-price shock and a global recession . . . caused commodity prices to fall into an extended slump."
The World Bank

✖ "Governments of poor countries should have [focused on] increased generation of foreign exchange to meet future obligations for debt service. On the contrary, most developing countries adopted [types of government] that resulted in expanded public sectors."
P. Kalonga Stambuli, University of Surrey

✖ "Tanzania, industrializing countries such as Brazil, Mexico, or Greece, and even wealthy nations such as Sweden, borrowed enormous sums of money abroad and squandered it. Why should the banks or other foreign lenders be expected to pay for the corruption, incompetence, and lack of foresight of underdeveloped politicians?"
Christie Davies, National Review

MORE TO THINK ABOUT

The debt crisis has an important influence on the relationship between developed and developing countries in the world. What might the consequences be if the debt was not paid back? How much does the original reason for the debt still matter?

Q: Will debt relief help developing countries?

WHOEVER IS to blame for the debt crisis, it is the people living in poor countries who are most affected. When money is spent on debt repayments, there is less available for programs such as health and education, which may help people to get out of poverty in the long-term. However, poor countries may want to borrow again as they develop. The way in which they handle debts from the past may influence lenders' decisions over loans in the future.

Debt relief has led to the abolishment of school fees for primary education in the African countries of Uganda, Malawi, Zambia, and Tanzania (pictured). This means that children do not have to miss out on education because their parents are poor.

YES

✓ "Ireland supports, in principle, the cancellation of their debts. We see debt cancellation as an important contribution by donors in support of . . . commitments to democracy, the rule of law, the fight against corruption, and the protection of human rights."

Bertie Ahern, Prime Minister, Republic of Ireland

✓ "Countries that can't afford to provide basic healthcare, education, or shelter to their people have to use their pitiful resources, including, in many cases, all their aid flows, to repay debts typically racked up by authoritarian, unelected regimes long since gone."

Dr. Noreena Hertz, academic and author

✓ "The greatest barrier to economic recovery [in Africa] is the region's overwhelming debt burden. . . . Creditors—chiefly the International Monetary Fund and World Bank—impose harsh conditions, and investors shy away from countries with unsustainable debts."

The 50 Years is Enough Network

CONFLICTING EVIDENCE?

The World Bank and IMF Heavily Indebted Poor Countries (HIPC) initiative is aimed at providing debt relief for the 42 poorest countries with little prospect of meeting their debt repayments. HIPC was first developed in 1996 and reformed in 1999.

"[HIPC] deals with debt in a comprehensive way to give countries the possibility of exiting from unsustainable debt. It is very good news for the poor of the world."

James D. Wolfensohn, President of the World Bank at the time of the HIPC launch

-------------------⬇-------------------

The amount of debt that the 42 countries will still have left after HIPC commitments on debt relief are delivered: $34.8 billion.

❖ STATISTICALLY SPEAKING

• The cost of the United Kingdom (U.K.) canceling its "share" of the outstanding multilateral debt owed by the 42 Heavily Indebted Poor Countries is $5 per person per year over 10 years.
• Nigeria spent $326.6 million on building a new soccer stadium, which was more than its combined budget for health and education.

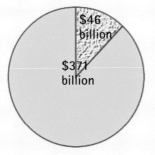

Original debt of the world's 42 poorest and most indebted countries

$46 billion

$371 billion

Amount of original debt actually written off by 2005

NO

"Countries need to . . . demonstrate to potential investors that they are sound places to invest. But if all of their debt is canceled, these countries may lose their credibility. In the long-term, this will make it difficult for countries to borrow money and attract foreign investors."
The World Bank

✖ "The challenge in places like Africa is to produce growth, which requires not just debt relief, but good policies, supported by effective and predictable aid flows, and open markets for exports."
Vikram Nehru, Manager of the Heavily Indebted Poor Countries initiative at the World Bank

✖ "If some debt owed to the World Bank is written off, that means there is less money to give to others. And there are some very poor countries without debt, so you have got to be careful about being fair."
Clare Short, former U.K. Secretary of State for international development

MORE TO THINK ABOUT

What are the implications of developed countries giving aid to poor countries while at the same time asking for debt repayments?

FIND OUT MORE: www.imf.org www.jubileeusa.org/jubilee.cgi
www.worlddebtrelief.com www.worldrevolution.org

Q: Do World Bank and IMF lending programs help poor countries?

THE WORLD Bank and the International Monetary Fund are two of the most powerful financial institutions in the world. They not only lend large amounts of money, but their involvement in a country also reassures other lenders. The World Bank and the IMF put conditions on their lending to ensure that loans are repaid. These conditions influence how the country runs its economy. They often include cuts in government spending, demands to open markets to foreign trade and investment, and privatization of state-run enterprises.

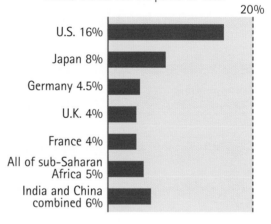

Voting rights at the World Bank
The number of shares a country has at the World Bank is based roughly on the size of its economy. Since 85 percent approval is required for major changes in World Bank policy, the United States has the power of veto.

- U.S. 16%
- Japan 8%
- Germany 4.5%
- U.K. 4%
- France 4%
- All of sub-Saharan Africa 5%
- India and China combined 6%

20%

YES "In some 60 low-income countries, these broad-based, country-led processes are taking hold and have helped promote a more open and inclusive national dialogue on the most effective policies and public actions for poverty reduction."
The World Bank and the IMF

✓ "There has been change. We are much more attentive to the question of growth and to the question of poverty reduction."
Simonetta Nardin, a senior external affairs officer at the IMF

✓ "In 1996, while visiting China, I met a woman from the Loess Plateau, where we supported an agricultural project. . . . Living in a cave, she had no power or running water, and had little prospect of improving her life. This spring, I had an emotional reunion with her, and she told me about how her life had improved, how she now has two caves, doors, windows, water, and power. How she had bought her son a motorcycle. . . . She was 1 of 3 million people who found hope through a series of 32 similar projects in the Plateau completed over 10 years."
James Wolfensohn, former President of the World Bank Group

NO "The poverty programs are expected to be consistent with . . . privatization, deregulation, budgetary constraints, and trade and financial liberalization. Yet these have [made worse the] economic and social crises in our countries."

Jubilee South Pan-African Declaration on the World Bank's and the IMF's lending conditions

✗ "Conditionality, at least in the manner and extent to which it has been used by the IMF, is a bad idea: there is little evidence that it leads to improved economic policy, but it does have adverse political effects because countries resent having conditions imposed upon them. . . . Studies at the World Bank and elsewhere showed not just that conditionality did not ensure that money was well spent and that countries would grow faster, but that there was little evidence it worked at all."

Joseph Stiglitz, former World Bank Senior Vice President

✗ "Now the common people are burdened to pay back such loans that have never benefited them in any way. They pay and pay and pay in the form of reduced healthcare, education, social services, deteriorating roads, and infrastructure."

Brother Andre, arrested after a demonstration at World Bank offices in Nairobi

✵ STATISTICALLY SPEAKING

• In 2004, the World Bank provided more than $19.4 billion for 245 projects in developing countries worldwide.
• Between 1987 and 1995, the IMF received around $3.5 billion more in debt repayments from the most indebted and impoverished countries than it provided.

Argentina, in South America, was once the world's seventh-largest economy, but by 2001, it was practically bankrupt. Some accused the IMF of making problems worse by insisting that the government make budget cuts that led to job and wage cuts. The sign on this shop reads, "Unfortunately, we've reached the end. Huge closing-down sale."

MORE TO THINK ABOUT

Do you think it is fair to put conditions (such as restricting a country's spending and asking it to open its trading markets) on a loan? Should countries be allowed to have loans without any conditions?

FIND OUT MORE: www.worldbank.org www.bicusa.org
www.globalexchange.org/campaigns/wbimf/faq.html

Q: Would a tax on the global flow of money benefit developing countries?

HUGE AMOUNTS of money flow between different countries each day as different currencies are bought and sold. The value of these currencies changes all the time. For example, the amount of U.S. dollars you could buy with one euro last year, or even last week, may well be different today. While this trading (called speculating) can be profitable, it can also have a destabilizing effect. Countries can have trouble if the value of their currency suddenly falls, or if large amounts of investment are withdrawn. Speculation has been blamed for upsetting Thailand's economy in 1997 and Brazil's in 1999. Some suggest that a tax on the global flow of money may limit this.

NO

"A [tax on the global flow of money] would be harmful to international trade, economic growth and welfare, and businesses throughout the world. The smallest nations would be most hurt. The tax would not prove feasible in practice since it would require uniform implementation throughout the world."

International Chamber of Commerce

"If the goal is to apply [a currency transaction tax] in countries that are particularly vulnerable to capital flight, then the danger is that it will make short-term borrowing, usually an emergency measure, much more difficult to acquire. If the goal is to generate aid for development purposes, then it is not at all clear that throwing sand into the financial system is the right way to do it."

U.K. House of Lords Select Committee on Economic Affairs

✪ STATISTICALLY SPEAKING

• Before 1970, 90 percent of international trade was in goods and services, and only 10 percent was in currencies. Today, the trade in currencies (with no direct link to particular goods or services) makes up 90 percent of transactions.

• The dollar, euro, yen, and pound together account for more than 75 percent of the financial exchange market. Developing country currencies make up only about 5 percent of the market.

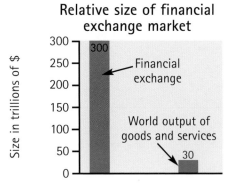

Relative size of financial exchange market

Size in trillions of $

- 300 — Financial exchange
- 30 — World output of goods and services

YES

"This House . . . believes that a small levy on such currency speculation . . . could both dampen down the scale and scope of speculation and raise substantial [money], potentially in excess of $50 billion each year, for projects targeted toward ending global poverty."

U.K. Parliament Early Day Motion

"There is no evidence that a 0.1 percent tax, for example, would have a negative impact on the international funding of goods and services. . . . In fact, the stability brought by the tax could contribute to a healthier financial environment for companies that exchange real goods and services."

Glyn Ford and Harlem Desir, Japan Times

"It is true, to talk of taxing financial transactions is a utopia. But we believe that this utopia must become reality. We need political regulation of financial globalization."

Gérard Fuchs, Member of Parliament, France

Imagine a stack of £50 notes reaching from the Earth to the Moon...

It's what the money trade is worth each year — two hundred thousand billion pounds

Now consider what a tiny tax on this astronomical amount could do...

Taxing the trade in currencies can bring millions of people out of poverty now

Currency trading is worth $353 trillion per year. This poster was created by an organization that believes a tax on currency trading could benefit developing countries.

MORE TO THINK ABOUT

Who might oversee any tax on the global flow of money?
How would decisions be made about what happens to the money raised?

FIND OUT MORE: www.stampoutpoverty.org www.attac.org
www.currencytax.org www.cttcampaigns.info

Q: Will more aid help developing countries?

DEVELOPED COUNTRIES try to reduce poverty through aid donations to developing countries. This is given through government aid agencies and institutions such as the World Bank, or by individuals making donations through organizations such as Oxfam. But some people are concerned that aid doesn't tackle poverty and that other measures work better.

Aid has been very important in eradicating global diseases. Since the 1960s, more than $88 million has been targeted to eradicate smallpox. This goal was reached worldwide by 1980.

YES

"For all developing countries, the amount of aid they receive and how it is spent is a critical part of their efforts to reduce poverty."

Oxfam International

✔ "If we are to achieve the Millennium Goals [see page 43], the heaviest responsibility inevitably must fall on the advanced economies. . . . They must meet their commitment to provide higher levels of aid, whenever possible on grant terms. Current aid flows are insufficient, unpredictable, and often uncoordinated among donors."

Rodrigo de Rato y Figadero, IMF Managing Director

✔ "One of the best ways to reduce poverty is by investing in people to achieve self-sufficiency. Aid provides targeted funds for . . . new crop varieties and irrigation, and provides education, research, and immunization."

Helen Hughes, senior fellow at The Center for Independent Studies in Sydney, Australia

✜ STATISTICALLY SPEAKING

• Sub-Saharan Africa receives more than $8.8 billion in aid every year but has to pay back at least this amount in debt repayments.

• Between 1960 and 1965, developed countries spent on average 0.48 percent of their combined national incomes on aid. By 1985, they were spending just 0.34 percent. By 2003, the average had dropped to 0.24 percent.

In 1970, the United Nations decided that 0.7 percent of Gross Domestic Product (GDP—a measure of a country's wealth) should be given as aid by developed countries. Very few countries actually meet this target.

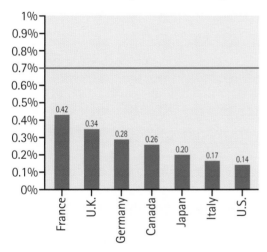

Source: compiled by Oxfam from Development Assistance Committee data, 2003

	Aid promised	Aid delivered by 2005
Earthquake in Iran, 2004	$1 billion	$17.6 million
Floods in Mozambique, 2000	$399 million	less than half
Hurricane Mitch in Honduras and Nicaragua, 1988	$8.8 billion	less than a third

NO

"Aid is a significant part of the problem, not a solution. Billions of multilateral and bilateral aid dollars, paying lip service to 'good policies,' have kept in power governments that rob and pillage their citizens."

Lyn Arnold, Chief Executive, World Vision Australia

✗ "The aid policies of donor countries are heavily influenced by politically powerful transnational corporations. These corporations' key interest is not in responding to need. Rather, it is in finding new markets to promote their goods."

Web site of "After the Tsunami" TV show, U.K.

CASE STUDY

THAILAND

In the wake of the 2004 tsunami, Thailand's prime minister followed India in announcing that his country did not want financial aid. Instead, he asked the European Union to lift trade tariffs on shrimp exports. He argued that these tariffs had cost his country far more than the amount promised by governments in emergency aid.

MORE TO THINK ABOUT

Some countries have asked for "trade not aid," although others have said that this could be used as an excuse by developed countries to cut back on promised aid. What might be the impact on your country if it gave more in aid?

FIND OUT MORE: www.oxfam.org www.un.org
www.cnn.com/SPECIALS/2004/tsunami.disaster www.worldvision.ca/home/index.cfm

Q: Should countries with civil wars still be given aid?

WHEN A country is experiencing a civil war, those who suffer the most are ordinary people who may have to leave their homes. During a civil war, governments often do not help people who they suspect are supporting their enemies. Such a situation is complicated for aid donors. For example, aid given to a government may not reach the right people or could even be used to buy weapons for the war.

YES

"We believe that even in conflict, all people should be able to live free of violence and coercion, and they should have the things they need to survive, including humanitarian relief."

Oxfam International

"Dark clouds are already gathering over the ideal that aid should be exclusively directed toward those that need it most. . . . World leaders must ensure that aid is not hijacked by the imperatives of the war on terror, as it was by the Cold War."

Christian Aid

NO

"I do not believe that anyone in the U.K. believes we should be providing long-term assistance to a country that is increasing its spending on arms year after year."

Clare Short, former U.K. Secretary of State for international development

"The U.S. government's apparent use of its aid efforts in Indonesia to solidify working relations with the Indonesian military (TNI), including the use of U.S. helicopters by the TNI, may only contribute to strengthening the position of the highly abusive military forces in that conflicted nation."

Tom Barry, International Relations Center

"Somalia, for example, and Rwanda are long-term recipients of American foreign aid, and it still didn't prevent their civil wars. And then we rushed in there with more foreign aid after the crisis, and conditions there are really not all that much better."

Bryan Johnson, policy analyst, Heritage Foundation

✿ STATISTICALLY SPEAKING
• More than 90 percent of the 150 wars fought between the end of World War II (1939–45) and the mid-1990s occurred in developing countries.

BURUNDI

When civil war broke out in Burundi, Africa, nearly all of the rural residents were forced to leave their homes and live in camps. People could not grow or sell crops, and farm animals died or were stolen. It was difficult for aid agencies to distribute aid during fighting, and soldiers would sometimes loot the camps for food. However, aid agencies did manage to set up water sources and medical centers. Aid agencies also helped people rebuild their houses after leaving the camps so that life could begin to return to normal.

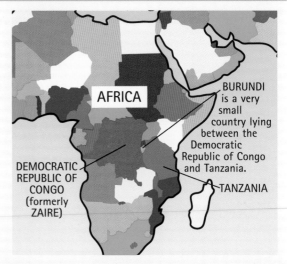

AFRICA

BURUNDI is a very small country lying between the Democratic Republic of Congo and Tanzania.

DEMOCRATIC REPUBLIC OF CONGO (formerly ZAIRE)

TANZANIA

At least two million people were affected by food shortages and homelessness during the civil war in the region of Darfur, in Sudan, Africa, in 2003–04.

MORE TO THINK ABOUT

In this section, we have seen the difficulties of helping people caught up in civil war. When, if ever, should other countries get involved to help people? Should they still stay to help if a situation worsens, or should they leave if they cannot make a difference?

FIND OUT MORE: www.christian-aid.org   www.amnesty.org
www.globalsecurity.org/military/world/war/sudan.htm

Q: Should the U.S. lead the way in reducing trade restrictions?

THE U.S. has massive influence over the way in which world trade works. It is among the world's biggest traders, and it plays an important role in developing global trade policies at the World Trade Organization (WTO). The U.S. government states that it is in favor of reducing barriers and allowing trade to take place freely between countries. However, some say that the U.S. needs to reduce its own trade barriers if its actions are to match its words.

Filipino protesters burn a sign in front of the U.S. embassy in Manila during a World Trade Organization meeting. The WTO sets the rules for global trade. It has been criticized for insisting that developing countries open up their economies to foreign imports while allowing developed countries to put up trade barriers.

YES

"Blind pursuit of U.S. economic and corporate special interests represents an obstacle to the creation of an international trading system capable of extending the benefits of globalization to the world's poor."
Kevin Watkins, Oxfam International

"[The U.S. and the EU] subsidize their agricultural producers, ignoring the rules of the WTO. Such practices are undermining the fragile national economies of countries that depend on cotton."
President Blaise Compaore of Burkina Faso

"[U.S. steel tariffs don't] help to persuade developing countries to open up their markets to free trade, one of the best ways for them to become more prosperous. The U.S. is causing great cynicism in these countries."
Digby Jones, Director-General of the Confederation of British Industry (CBI)

NO "We will be defending U.S. agricultural interests in every form we need to and have no intention of unilaterally disarming."

Neena Moorjani, spokeswoman for the U.S. Trade Representative's office on a U.S. appeal against a WTO ruling that subsidies paid to U.S. cotton farmers violated global trade rules

"We have to recognize that our trade and manufacturing crisis has become so grave that we have no choice but to start thinking seriously about restricting trade in various ways."

Alan Tonelson, U.S. Business and Industry Council

CONFLICTING EVIDENCE?

"My administration is promoting free and fair trade."

U.S. President George W. Bush, 2004 State of the Union address

In March 2002, the U.S. imposed 30 percent tariffs on foreign steel products from Europe and other nations.

The U.S. said that it was a necessary move to protect its steel industry. Critics suggested that the role of steel unions in key states in an upcoming election was behind the decision, as the price of steel was rising anyway.

The tariffs were lifted after trading partners threatened retaliation against U.S. exports.

"Unfair foreign pricing and government subsidies distort the free flow of goods and adversely affect American business in the global marketplace."

U.S. Import Administration

✳ STATISTICALLY SPEAKING

• The poorest 49 countries make up 10 percent of the world's population but only account for 0.4 percent of world trade.

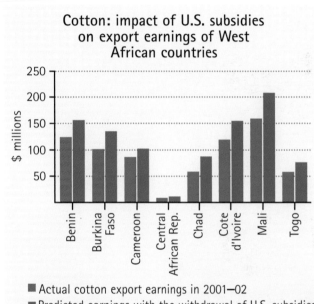

Cotton: impact of U.S. subsidies on export earnings of West African countries

$ millions

■ Actual cotton export earnings in 2001–02
■ Predicted earnings with the withdrawal of U.S. subsidies

MORE TO THINK ABOUT

In practice, even countries that promote free trade may subsidize certain industries. When countries use this practice, it makes it even harder for developing countries to catch up in the global trading system.

FIND OUT MORE: www.ustr.gov www.twnside.org.sg
www.usda.govecedweb.unomaha.edu/lessons/feoga.htm

Q: Does fair trade help developing countries?

FAIR TRADE occurs when standards for trade are set with environmental and social goals in mind. It is a long-term approach to tackling poverty and usually includes a guarantee of a decent price for farmers' crops. Fair trade companies may buy directly from farmers so that money goes back to the communities that produce the goods, rather than to a "middle man." Only a tiny amount of consumer goods overall are fairly traded.

YES

"Fair traders believe that their system of trade, based on respect for workers' rights and the environment, if adopted by the big players in the global economy, can play a big part in reversing the growing inequities and environmental degradation that have accompanied the growth in world trade."

John Cavanagh, Institute for Policy Studies

"Fair trade is better than aid or charity—it can help directly in building a sustainable future based on producers' own skills and resources rather than continuing dependency on handouts."

Equal Exchange

"The difference fair trade cocoa makes for me is that . . . I know I will have a market. I know that I will be able to sell my cocoa. By having that assurance, I can make plans. If I want to buy books for the children's studies or we want to take a trip, we can plan for that."

Justino Peck, Toledo Cacao Growers Association, Belize

✤ STATISTICALLY SPEAKING

• The U.K. is the biggest fair trade market in the world. Sales topped $247 million in 2004—a 51 percent rise from 2003.
• At least five million people, including farmers, workers, and their families across 49 developing countries, benefit from the International Fairtrade Foundation's trading system.

The money that farmers make from coffee can only buy one-quarter of what it could buy 40 years ago and is the lowest real price farmers have been paid in 100 years.

How much coffee does it take to buy a Swiss Army knife?

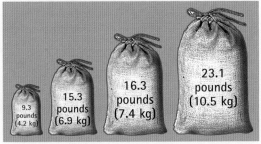

| 1980 | 1990 | 2000 | 2001 |

9.3 pounds (4.2 kg) — 1980
15.3 pounds (6.9 kg) — 1990
16.3 pounds (7.4 kg) — 2000
23.1 pounds (10.5 kg) — 2001

CASE STUDY

GRASSROOTS HQ

In 1991, a group of women from San Patong, in northern Thailand, set up Grassroots HQ, a fair trade company that makes paper and stationery products. The products are sold all over the world. Craftswomen have been making paper from mulberry tree bark in the area for 700 years. It is a sustainable way to make money from forest resources. The women do not have to leave to work in cities because they can now earn a fair wage by working in their village.

NO

"Fair trade isn't a viable solution. . . . First, it favors the few, and, secondly, it provides an incentive to farmers to increase coffee production at a time when they should perhaps be seriously considering alternative crops."

Gordon Gillet, Senior Vice President for purchasing and exports, Nestlé

✘ "If we buy our chocolate based on a combination of taste and price, the 'best' chocolate producers will be rewarded and can expand. This is the market. If we value other things, like the wages of the workers who produced the chocolate, we could end up being counterproductive by initiating an artificial wage floor, which creates unemployment and misdirected resources."

Posting to blog on The Filter Web site

✘ "The fair trade movement will have to confront the possibility that organizing labor across a whole sector to face up to [low pay and working] pressures may do more good than singling out individual producers and asking consumers to pay more."

Felicity Lawrence, journalist

MORE TO THINK ABOUT

Fair trade goods help the small farmers who can sell their goods in this way, but what about all of the other goods we buy? Fair trade goods usually cost more to buy. Why do you think some people are prepared to pay more? How would you feel about it?

FIND OUT MORE: www.maketradefair.com www.fairtradefederation.com
www.wto.org www.transfairusa.org

Q: Do free trade zones benefit host countries?

FREE TRADE zones (FTZs), also known as export processing zones, are special areas of a country where restrictions on businesses, such as taxes, tariffs, and labor laws, do not apply. Many countries have created FTZs to encourage companies to set up factories in their country and provide jobs for workers. Because companies in FTZs do not have to follow the normal laws of a country, they have been accused of exploiting workers by not allowing them to join trade unions, paying low wages, and making people work in poor conditions.

YES

"In order to stimulate rapid economic growth of the country, particularly through industrialization, the government has adopted an 'Open Door Policy' to attract foreign investment to Bangladesh."

Bangladesh Export Processing Zones Authority

"The FTZ provides special tax advantages that are aimed to attract foreign and local investment that will not be present in their absence. Basically, the government foregoes receipt of income from duties and, possibly, other taxes in order to encourage investments."

Dr. Simon Hakim and Dr. Erwin A. Blackstone, Privatization Research Center

CASE STUDY

MEXICO

In Mexico, the last 30 years have seen FTZs created along the border with the U.S. The factories and plants where the goods are assembled are known as "maquilas." They produce mainly clothes, car parts, and electronic goods.

In one area, the Tehuacán Valley, so many indigenous people have moved to work in the maquilas that the area is known as the "City of Indians." The wages are more than double what people would earn in their traditional work as farmers. However, because so many young people have left to work in the maquilas, there are not enough people to work in the fields. The traditional indigenous communities feel they have lost their youth, culture, and identity.

"For Nicaraguan women, having a job in the FTZs means not having to sell food and trinkets in the streets and also not having to leave the country to become maids in Costa Rica. The reality is that there are no jobs in other sectors in Nicaragua."

Rose-Marie Avin, participant in January 2002 study tour with Wisconsin Coordinating Council on Nicaragua

✳ STATISTICALLY SPEAKING

• By 2001, 800,000 new jobs had been created in FTZs along the U.S. border. However, in the next 3 years or so, 500,000 workers lost their jobs as multinational companies moved their operations to countries with even cheaper labor.

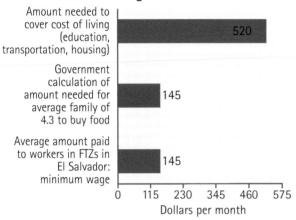

Worker's wages in El Salvador

	Dollars per month
Amount needed to cover cost of living (education, transportation, housing)	520
Government calculation of amount needed for average family of 4.3 to buy food	145
Average amount paid to workers in FTZs in El Salvador: minimum wage	145

An employee in a factory in a free trade zone in El Salvador. The factory makes clothes for the U.S. supermarket Wal-Mart.

NO

"What these rulers mean by 'development' is the increase of their own wealth and power."

Dan Gallin, Global Labor Institute

✖ "Workers, mostly women, seek work in the zones for their own economic security and to contribute financially to their families. Work inside the zones is often more highly paid than outside. However, the intensity of work is high, the quality of jobs poor, and repression of basic rights is widespread."

From "Effective Strategies In Confronting Transnational Corporations," edited by Abdul Aziz Choudry

✖ "Some women noted that years of working in the FTZs left them with poor eyesight and breathing problems, rendering them virtually unemployable."

Women's Edge Coalition

MORE TO THINK ABOUT

FTZs raise issues about the rights and responsibilities of companies. Is what seems to be good for the economy always good for wider society? In what other ways do developing countries attract investment and create jobs in today's world?

FIND OUT MORE: www.maquilasolidarity.org   www.codezol.com
www.freezones.ir   www.kishtpc.com/Freetrade%20ZONES.htm

Q: Would a World Parliament narrow the gap between rich and poor?

THE WORLD'S developed countries dominate the key international financial organizations of the World Bank and the IMF, the international trade organization of the WTO, and the international political body of the UN. This seems unfair: a possible solution might be to develop a new institution, a World Parliament, to allow fairer representation of all of the world's citizens—rich and poor —in addressing key issues. But this might be unworkable and unnecessary—if we could reform existing institutions.

NO "There is little evidence that a sufficiently strong sense of community exists at the global level [on which to build a parliament]."

Joseph Nye, Harvard University

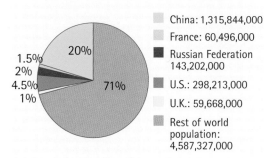 "Democracy remains rooted in local communities and nation-states. So it is difficult to work together internationally . . . without leaving voters feeling out of touch. . . . Nor are world elections to a world parliament and a world government realistic. Sixty million Britons would not accept 1.3 billion Chinese outvoting them."

Philippe Legrain, former special adviser to the Director-General of the World Trade Organization

How world population is split between different continents

5% 1% 14% 9% 11% 60%

Africa: 905,936,000
Asia: 3,905,415,000
Europe: 728,389,000
Latin America and the Caribbean: 561,346,000
North America: 330,608,000
Oceania: 33,056,000

How world population is split between the populations of the five permanent members of the United Nations Security Council and the rest of world population

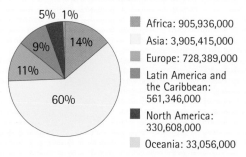

20% 1.5% 2% 4.5% 1% 71%

China: 1,315,844,000
France: 60,496,000
Russian Federation 143,202,000
U.S.: 298,213,000
U.K.: 59,668,000
Rest of world population: 4,587,327,000

Source: UN Department of Economic and Social Affairs

A row of flags from some of the countries that are members of the United Nations. The role of the UN is often a subject of debate. Some want it to play a greater role in world affairs, while others would like to see its involvement reduced.

YES

"We in the rich world live in comparative comfort only because of the inordinate power our governments wield. . . . The absence of an accountable forum does not prevent global decision-making from taking place—it merely ensures that it does not take place democratically."

George Monbiot, author of
The Age of Consent

"Unfortunately, we have no world government, accountable to the people of every country, to oversee the globalization process in a fashion comparable to the way national governments guided the nationalization process."

Joseph Stiglitz, former Chief Economist at the World Bank

"It is sometimes said that we are not ready for such a world democracy, but we already live in an overwhelmingly democratic world. . . . The majority of the inhabitants of our small blue planet are living under governments that they have chosen."

Coalition for a World Parliament and World Democracy

MORE TO THINK ABOUT

Finding ways to hold accountable one organization representing the world's six billion people would be quite a challenge. Also, if voting were based on population figures, then China and India alone would be able to act together to impose policies upon the rest of the world.

FIND OUT MORE: www.tgde.org   www.world-democracy.org
www.un.org/Docs/sc/

Q: Will genetically modified crops solve world hunger?

A scientist carries out an experiment with genetically modified rice at the International Rice Research Institute in the Philippines.

CHRONIC HUNGER is still a problem for approximately 852 million people worldwide. While there may be enough food in the world for everyone, clearly not everyone is getting access to it. Genetically modified (GM) crops that can grow in degraded environments have been proposed as one solution to the problem of too little available food. To date, most of the GM crops in the world have been grown for animal feed and for consumption in developed countries.

YES

✓ "Environmental stresses pose ever more serious threats to global agricultural production and food security. . . . Anything we can do to help crop plants cope with environmental stresses will also raise the quality and quantity of food for those who need it most."

Professor Ray Wu, Cornell University, speaking about his research on drought-tolerant rice

✓ "The use of high-yielding, disease-resistant, and pest-resistant crops would have a direct bearing on improved food security, poverty alleviation, and environmental conservation in Africa."

Dr. John Wafula of the Kenya Agricultural Research Institute

✓ "It would be unethical to condemn future generations to hunger by refusing to develop and apply a technology that can build on what our forefathers provided and can help produce adequate food for a world with almost two billion more people by 2020."

Richard Flavell, biologist

- The International Food Policy Research Institute estimates that global food production must increase by 40 percent in the next 20 years for a better and more varied diet for the predicted population of 8 billion people.
- World grain yields grew more quickly in the 1980s and '90s than the population did, rising by 2.2 percent a year while the world population grew by 1.7 percent each year.

NO "We strongly object that the image of the poor and hungry from our countries is being used by giant multinational corporations to push [GM crops]. . . . We think it will destroy the diversity, the local knowledge, and the sustainable agricultural systems. . . . It will thus undermine our capacity to feed ourselves."

Statement from all of the African delegates (except South Africa) to the UN's Food and Agriculture Organization

✖ "Farmers today produce far less than they could with presently available know-how and technology because there is no incentive for them to do so—there are only low prices and few buyers. No new seed, good or bad, can change that."

Peter Rosset, Codirector, Food First, Institute for Food and Development Policy

✖ "[GM crops] are driven by commercial interests, not a concern to 'feed the world' or raise productivity. The real challenge is poverty eradication."

Andrew Simms, Christian Aid

CASE STUDY

ZAMBIA

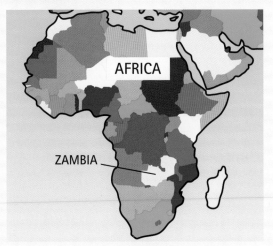

In 2002, 2.9 million Zambians were in need of food. Food aid, half of which was donated by the U.S. and contained GM food, was headed for Zambia. But the Zambian president rejected it. His reasoning was that if cross-pollination occurred, it could hurt future exports to Europe, where there is opposition to GM foods. "We may be poor," he said, "but we aren't ready to expose our people to ill-defined risks." Lovemore Simwanda of the Zambian National Farmers Union said: "[The American government] thinks we've got hunger and that we're going to be forced into accepting their food and ultimately GM."

MORE TO THINK ABOUT
This section covers key issues of population, food aid, and choice of crops.

A further area to consider is: should patents on GM foods apply in developing countries?

27

Q: Should Western consumerism be a model for developing countries?

As BIG businesses extend their trade, the diets, recreational practices, and lifestyles of Western consumers are being practiced in more countries around the world. While consumer goods should not be limited to developed countries, Western lifestyles have proved to be a severe drain on the environment. Also, despite high consumption, countries in the West still suffer from problems such as ill health, crime, and a growing divide between rich and poor.

YES "Consuming produces good government. Consumer societies are those in which people make and spend money freely, and on a large scale. . . . Wealth produces better government, and better government produces wealth."
Richard D. North, commentator

"In general, the developing countries that have increased their participation in [international] trade and attracted foreign investment have accelerated growth and reduced poverty."
David Dollar, Director of Developmental Policy at the World Bank

"The global market economy has demonstrated great productive capacity. Wisely managed, it can deliver unprecedented material progress, generate more productive and better jobs for all, and contribute significantly to reducing world poverty."
International Labor Organization

NO "Beyond its knowledge and its highly celebrated 'discoveries,' Western society corrupts as it consumes. It also forgets and underestimates the wisdom of other cultures—a wisdom it never attempted to comprehend."
Juan Rivera Tosi, Mosaico 21 magazine

"The wealthier consume precisely because others are poor—the rich consume at the expense of the poor."
Anup Shah, Global Issues

"Western patterns of consumption as the basis of development for, say, China or India—adding another two billion 'Western-style' consumers—is simply not a realistic option unless the risk of catastrophic collapse of the global ecosystem is considered acceptable."
United Nations Environment Program

• The average U.S. citizen uses nearly 9 times more energy than the average person in China and 12 times more than the average person in Africa.

• A 2004 report found that humanity is using more than 20 percent more natural resources than Earth can regenerate (source: WWF).

Annual expenditure on luxury items compared with funding needed to meet selected basic needs

Product	Annual Expenditure	Social or Economic Goal	Additional Annual Investment Needed to Achieve Goal
Makeup	$17.6 billion	Reproductive healthcare for all women	$12 billion
Pet food in Europe and U.S.	$16.7 billion	Elimination of hunger and malnutrition	$19.4 billion
Perfumes	$15 billion	Universal literacy	$5.3 billion
Ocean cruises	$14 billion	Clean drinking water for all	$9.7 billion
Ice cream in Europe	$10.6 billion	Immunizing every child	$1.3 billion

Share of world private consumption spending

1.5% 1.4%
2.0% 1.2%
3.3%
6.7%
31.5%
21.4%
28.7%

Share of world population

10.9% 5.2%
4.1% 6.4%
0.4%
22.4% 32.9%
7.9% 8.5%

U.S. and Canada
Western Europe
East Asia and Pacific
Latin America and the Caribbean
Eastern Europe and Central Asia

South Asia
Australia and New Zealand
Middle East and North Africa
Sub-Saharan Africa

In 2004, activists in Denmark celebrated "Buy Nothing Day" with a "Santa says stop shopping" demonstration in Copenhagen's busiest shopping street. Dressed as Santa and elves, the activists handed out flyers to passing shoppers, encouraging them to cut their consumption levels.

MORE TO THINK ABOUT
How do consumption habits change as society changes? Will increasing claims about limited resources be seen as a threat to the way of life of those who currently consume more?

Q: Can celebrity-led campaigns make a difference?

FEW INTERNATIONAL campaigns on poverty seem complete these days without celebrity backing. This can benefit the celebrities by increasing their personal profile. It can benefit campaigns by attracting media attention and exposing a whole new audience to important issues. Young people in particular may be more likely to show an interest in issues of global poverty if their favorite pop star sees it as important.

The rock star Bono speaking to European Union leaders about the importance of doubling aid to developing countries. Bono has shared a platform with world leaders, including former U.S. President Bill Clinton, President Thabo Mbeki of South Africa, and British Prime Minister Tony Blair.

YES

"Bono and I are under no illusions. We have the ability to articulate the great wound of the 21st century and have access to politicians."

Sir Bob Geldof, singer and celebrity activist

"Some people think musicians should stick with the music. I cringe when I see a celebrity with a cause—and I am one! But when two and a half million people in Africa will die of AIDS this year, we are not talking about a 'cause'—we are talking about an emergency, a global humanitarian emergency. . . . The most I can do as a musician is raise the alarm."

Bono, singer

"Rock and movie stars have their purpose. They guarantee good photo opportunities, front page coverage, and show the MTV generation that the World Economic Forum can't be so bad after all."

Tim Weber, BBC Business Editor

✺ STATISTICALLY SPEAKING

• Time taken by actress Sharon Stone to raise $1 million for mosquito nets from an audience of business leaders at the 2005 World Economic Forum:

10 minutes

• Money raised at the January 2005 WaveAid concert in Australia for the 2004 tsunami benefit appeal:

$2.5 million

CASE STUDY

MAKE POVERTY HISTORY

Celebrities were at the forefront of the Make Poverty History campaign, which called on the Group of 8 (G8) leaders to address global poverty at their meeting in 2005. Afterward, celebrity activist and rock singer Bob Geldof described the G8 meeting as a "mission accomplished." However, some organizations and activists from poorer countries believed that Geldof overrated the meeting. They said that he was not qualified to publicly declare whether the G8 leaders should be congratulated or condemned.

"We are very critical of what Bob Geldof did during the G8 Summit," said Demba Moussa Dembele of the African Forum on Alternatives. "The objectives of the whole Live8 campaign had little to do with poverty reduction in Africa. It was a program intended to project Geldof and [British Prime Minister Tony] Blair as humanitarian figures coming to the rescue of 'poor and helpless' Africans."

NO "It's sometimes hard to hear [TV presenters or pop stars] preach about child poverty and assume an air of moral superiority when you're surrounded by pictures of them cavorting on beaches or coming out of expensive restaurants."

Virginia Featherston, brand agency director

✖ "Political opinion tends to run deep, and one celebrity is unlikely to change that in any but the most fickle and truly undecided."

Robert Thompson, Syracuse University, on celebrity involvement in the U.S. presidential election

✖ "Nobody I know thinks entertainers are any more informed than, say, cab drivers, accountants, or cashiers. Nor do I know anybody who thinks that the mastery of one craft grants an exalted status to a person's views on entirely unrelated subjects. In fact, most people seem to recognize that the words of outspoken celebrities are of very little political consequence."

Evan Coyne Maloney, Brain Terminal

MORE TO THINK ABOUT

Making international poverty and trade issues interesting can be quite a challenge for activists. Meanwhile, it can be a challenge for celebrity activists to ensure that judgments on their artistic merit are kept separate from judgments on their political stance. Should they just stick to what they are best at?

FIND OUT MORE: www.makepovertyhistory.org www.weforum.org
www.live8insider.com www.bonoonline.com

Q: Has the developed world's failure to tackle poverty led to terrorism?

COUNTRIES AROUND the world are increasingly concerned about terrorism, particularly since the 2001 attacks on New York and Washington, D.C. Terrorism has been applied loosely to a wide variety of situations, making it difficult to get to root causes. Some people have suggested that motivating factors may have come from global poverty, including frustration at the unfair distribution of food and the poor quality of life in many countries.

The causes and significance of the 2001 attack on the Twin Towers in New York have been much debated.

YES

"Poverty, disease, and environmental decline are the true axes of evil. Unless the world takes action to improve economic and environmental conditions around the world, security officials will face an uphill battle in dealing with the many consequences of vulnerable societies—from wars and terrorism to heightened impacts from natural disasters."

Christopher Flavin, Worldwatch President

"When I got to the Gaza Strip, I could understand why this is the place where such strong resistance was born. . . . There is inadequate housing, sanitation, and education, and almost no jobs. Face it, wouldn't you be a little angry if you had grown up in such a situation?"

Abeja, The Odyssey World Trek

"The threats we face are threats to all of us. And they are linked to each other. We will not defeat terrorism unless we also tackle the causes of conflict and misgovernment in developing countries."

Kofi Annan, Secretary-General, United Nations

✳ STATISTICALLY SPEAKING

- World military expenditures are nearly $1 trillion a year.
- Worldwide, more than 200 million young people who are either jobless or do not earn enough to support a family—especially young men—can be a destabilizing force.
- Global income inequality is probably greater now than it has ever been in human history. Currently, the richest 1 percent of people in the world receive as much income as the whole of the bottom 57 percent.

Countries judged to be most at risk of terrorism

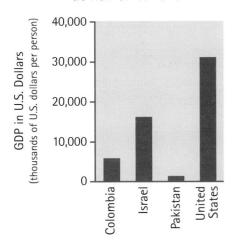

Total International Terror Attacks 1982–2003

The number of terrorist attacks has broadly decreased in the last 20 years.

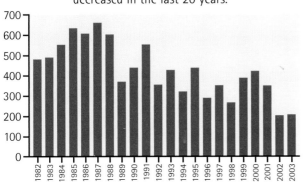

NO "Few terrorists are poor. The leaders of the September 11 group were all well-educated men, far from the bottom rungs of their societies."
Colin Powell, former U.S. Secretary of State

✖ "Why do they hate us? They hate what they see right here in this chamber—a democratically elected government. Their leaders are self-appointed. They hate our freedoms—our freedoms of religion, our freedom of speech, our freedom to vote and assemble and disagree with each other."
George W. Bush, U.S. President

✖ "The experts have maintained for a long time that poverty does not cause terrorism and prosperity does not cure it. In the world's 50 poorest countries, there is little or no terrorism."
Walter Laqueur, Cochair of the International Research Council at the Center for Strategic and International Studies

MORE TO THINK ABOUT

In this section, we have looked at issues surrounding terrorism, including income and democracy. Other issues to consider include:
- national independence
- ethnic tensions
- religion
- limited natural resources, such as water.

FIND OUT MORE: www.worldwatch.org state.gov/s/ct/
english.safe-democracy.org/causes www.cfrterrorism.org/causes

Q: Should developed countries pay for developing countries' environmental problems?

ONE OF the eight UN Millennium Development Goals (see page 43) states that without a healthy and secure environment, many of the other goals will be hard to achieve. However, who will pay for a secure environment? Some say that developed countries should pay, as much of the damage is a result of their activities, including high consumption of resources. Others say that people in developing countries have made choices about how they treat their local environment.

✱ STATISTICALLY SPEAKING

• Climate change could cost developing countries up to $11.5 trillion over the next 20 years, many times the amount of money anticipated as aid.
• Since 1991, the Global Environment Facility (run by the World Bank, the United Nations Environment Program, and the United Nations Development Program) has provided $4.4 billion in grants and helped raise $14 billion for projects in developing countries.
• High-income countries, with 15 percent of the world's population, use half of the energy in the world and produce more than half of the global emissions of carbon dioxide, one of the main greenhouse gases contributing to climate change.

YES

"The rich measure only financial debts. The cost to the environment and its value is not taken into account, even though that debt dwarfs all others. . . . The simplest example of this growing cost to the environment, for which the developing world pays the price, is burning fossil fuels. It should be regarded as a debt owed by the developed world."

Andrew Simms, New Economics Foundation

"The advanced countries and their corporations should pay compensation for damage that has already occurred in poor countries, as well as for measures designed to protect against future damage."

Magazine for Development and Cooperation

"As debts mounted, what poorer countries needed most was foreign currency to pay back their debts. One easy solution was to milk Earth's resources for the hard cash they brought in and cut back on environmental conservation programs."

Jubilee Research

CASE STUDY

TUVALU

The Pacific island state of Tuvalu is considered to be at high risk from the rising sea levels and storms associated with climate change. People in Tuvalu are worried about their country, and many have already left.

In 2002, Tuvalu's prime minister announced that he was considering legal action at the International Court of Justice. He proposed filing a suit against nations such as the U.S. and Australia— countries that emit the highest amounts of greenhouse gases. The suit was never filed because the prime minister failed to get reelected.

This picture shows Fongafale Island, the capital island of Tuvalu. The island's coastline can already be seen breaking up on the right. This makes it more vulnerable to flooding and erosion.

MORE TO THINK ABOUT

How do you put a price on environmental problems?
How do you find out just who is responsible?

NO

"The activists' recipe for solving global warming . . . appears to be . . . to have the developed world send what money it has left over to the developing world. It's not clear, though, that an economically crippled developed world would be able or willing to subsidize poor countries, leaving those countries forever impoverished."

Steven Milloy, journalist and academic

"I believe all countries have a responsibility to do something for the environment. . . . Poor countries have large human resources that they can mobilize. And they should go ahead and do so, without waiting for the rich countries to do something. . . . Poor countries must stop always acting like rich countries are the big brother, like they cannot do anything until the rich countries do it. . . . And then you can put pressure on big countries to play their part."

Wangari Maathai, Deputy Environment Minister, Kenya

FIND OUT MORE: www.neweconomics.org   www.foei.org
www.gefweb.org   www.climate.org

Q: Does having natural resources make a country rich?

Natural RESOURCES are an important source of income for many developing countries. Natural resources are raw materials such as oil, minerals, and timber. Since these resources are worth large sums of money, it would seem likely that the countries in which they are found would be rich. This, however, is not always the case.

✸ STATISTICALLY SPEAKING

• The proportion of people living on less than $1 a day in mineral-exporting countries rose from 61 percent in 1981 to 82 percent in 1999.
• In the 1990s, rebels, warlords, corrupt governments, and other groups earned an estimated $12 billion worldwide in revenues from marketing their countries' natural resources.

Poverty and resource dependence: the links

There are strong links between poor development indicators and countries' reliance on mineral and oil exports.

	Highly oil-dependent countries	Highly mineral-dependent countries
Low Human Development Index ranking	🛢	💎
Population in poverty		💎
High under-five mortality	🛢	💎
Low life expectancy		💎
High income inequality		💎
Authoritarianism	🛢	💎
Likelihood of civil war	🛢	💎
High military spending	🛢	💎

YES ✓ "With . . . vast human and natural resources, a revitalized Nigeria can be the economic and political anchor of West Africa."
Bill Clinton, former U.S. President

✓ "It would be natural to assume that the Philippines' rich endowment of mineral wealth would have translated into increased prosperity for all. [The Philippine government] says that mining companies have provided employment, either directly or indirectly, and that some of the most remote regions have benefited economically, citing direct or indirect employment and the economic stimulation of some remote regions."
Christian Aid and PIPLinks

✓ "Natural resources-based activities can lead growth for long periods of time. This is patently evident in the development history of natural resource-rich developed countries, such as Australia, Finland, Sweden, and the U.S. Mining was the main driver of growth and industrialization in Australia and the U.S. over more than a century."
The World Bank

CASE STUDY

"DUTCH DISEASE"

"Dutch disease" is named after a phenomenon that took place in the Netherlands following the discovery of natural gas. It is not uncommon in countries with natural resources. The pattern goes as follows: When the natural resource is discovered and sold, the value of the country's currency rises compared to the currencies of other countries. This makes the country's other exports more expensive on the world market. Exports then fall, and exporting industries struggle. Imports increase to fill the gap, and the country becomes increasingly dependent on income from the one commodity that it knows it can sell—the natural resource.

Ninety percent of the Angolan government's income is from oil. Yet nearly two-thirds of the population has no access to safe drinking water, and the country ranks 151 out of 173 in global human development.

NO "We have seen the devastating effects of some of the mining operations. . . . The adverse social impact on the affected communities, especially on our indigenous brothers and sisters, far outweighs the gains promised by large-scale mining corporations."

Catholic Bishops' Conference of the Philippines

"We have oil and gas from our natural resources, and these belong to us. I read in the newspapers that foreigners get profit, and we just provide our labor. . . . It does make me angry that millions of dollars are being obtained in oil, but we don't even have drinking water."

Svetlana Voitiva of Narynkol in eastern Kazakhstan

"Oil makes matters worse in countries where governments are already weak. It provides the income for a government to ignore its people and get on with the business of spending oil revenue without questions being asked."

Michael Ross, UCLA

MORE TO THINK ABOUT

Value is added to a natural resource when it is processed. However, tariffs on processed goods can be high. This prevents poorer countries from developing local industries to process and add value to raw materials. Such industries would also allow poorer countries to develop their economies overall.

Q: Should developed countries allow more immigration from developing countries?

THERE ARE many reasons why people move from one country to another. Some seek work, as there may be none at home. Some may be fleeing wars or persecution. Meanwhile, rich countries need immigrants for their workforces. Although a diverse society may be a healthy one, some suggest that increased immigration can put poor communities in developed countries under too much pressure.

YES

"There are currently 100,000 unfilled vacancies in food production in the U.K. The affluent British do not want these jobs. Economic immigrants do. I would like to employ many, many more, but the crazy immigration laws do not allow me to supply what my customers and, ultimately, the U.K. public want."

Comment posted during BBC Web site debate

"In most countries, [immigration controls] are less than 100 years old. International migration, on the other hand, has always existed. . . . Freedom of movement should be the new common sense."

Teresa Hayter, author of Open Borders

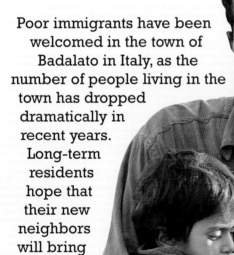

Poor immigrants have been welcomed in the town of Badalato in Italy, as the number of people living in the town has dropped dramatically in recent years. Long-term residents hope that their new neighbors will bring work, families, and a future to the town.

CASE STUDY

LONGER WORKING LIVES

In 2000, a United Nations report found that without increased immigration to developed countries, there would be an uneven ratio between working people and those expecting to retire. People would not be able to retire until they were at least 75 years old.

✸ STATISTICALLY SPEAKING

• In 2002, total migrant workers' remittances (money sent back to relatives) to developing countries amounted to $88 billion, which was about $30 billion more than official development assistance.

• By 2050, up to 150 million people may be displaced by the impacts of climate change and become refugees. These impacts include rising sea levels and unpredictable weather patterns.

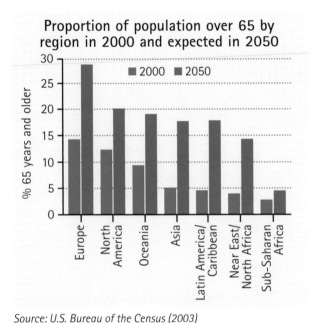

Proportion of population over 65 by region in 2000 and expected in 2050

Source: U.S. Bureau of the Census (2003)

CONFLICTING EVIDENCE?

Respondents to a 2003 poll estimated that 23 percent of the world's refugee population comes to the U.K.

⬇

The U.K. ranked ninth in Europe in terms of asylum applications per capita in 2003. At the end of 2003, the U.K. hosted around 270,000 refugees, 2.8 percent of the world's 9.7 million refugees, and 0.4 percent of the U.K. population.

NO "We should attempt to improve the situation in poor countries, rather than just allowing anyone with the drive to leave. This proposal will cause a brain drain of talent from the countries that most need it."

From an argument on the International Debate Education Association Web site

✖ "Any discussion of poverty in the U.S. would have to deal with immigration. . . . It doesn't make sense to import poverty."

Steven A. Camarota, Director of Research, Center for Immigration Studies, U.S. (an organization that wants stricter immigration limits)

✖ "It's not racist to want to limit the numbers. . . . Any system of immigration must be properly controlled. There are, literally, millions of people in other, poorer countries who would like to settle here if they could. Britain cannot possibly take them all."

Michael Howard, former leader of the Conservative Party, U.K.

MORE TO THINK ABOUT
Most refugees cannot afford to leave their regions of origin. Two-thirds of the world's refugees live in developing countries, and more than a third live in the world's poorest countries, many of them in refugee camps.

Q: Is there enough media coverage of poverty in developing countries?

FOR MOST of us, the media is the main source if information about what is going on in the world. The media is often accused of not providing enough coverage of poverty, or of trivializing the depth of the problem by only covering short-term crises. The media is subject to many pressures when choosing what to cover. These include editorial guidelines, advertising, and consumer interest.

YES

"A recent survey showed that the majority of young people growing from youth to adulthood in these years agreed that Live Aid was for them the single most memorable moment in their lives. And Live Aid started with an exposure by journalism and BBC [journalist] Michael Buerk's reports from Africa."

Gordon Brown, U.K. Chancellor of the Exchequer

"The Nick 2015 initiative makes the Millennium Campaign relevant to kids and empowers them to play a role in shaping their future."

Bill Roedy, Vice Chairman of MTV Networks and President of MTV Networks International, on TV plans to show how Millennium Development Goals [see page 43] affect young people

A cameraman films a refugee food line in Baidoa, Somalia.

NO "Traditional news values work against continued coverage of failing states. In addition, the structure and culture of the newsroom makes it likely that even in cases where there [is] some news to be told, it will not be told in any significant fashion."

Hans-Henrik Holm, Danish School of Journalism

✗ "The actual voices of poor people, especially women, are still rare. Stories are rarely framed from their vantage point. Thus, where poor people are quoted, it is to humanize the story, not to shape the overall perspective."

Guy Gough Berger, Rhodes University, South Africa

❋ STATISTICALLY SPEAKING

• A 2004 BBC online survey of 8,500 people worldwide found that 72 percent of respondents had never heard of the UN Millennium Development Goals.

• In the 1990s, evening news shows in the U.S. devoted 82 percent of the airtime given to foreign coverage to just 14 countries, or 7 percent of the world's total countries.

CONFLICTING EVIDENCE?

"Today, the electronic media and the Internet are important sources for breaking news to the public. As a result of the Internet, there is now an enormous amount of information available, also on humanitarian crises."

Hans-Henrik Holm, Danish School of Journalism

-------------------⊕-------------------

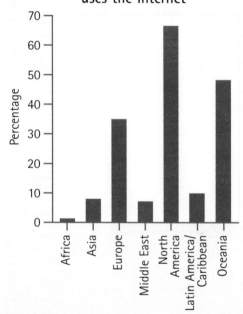

Percentage of population that uses the Internet

Number of articles in 23 newspapers (U.S. & Western Europe):

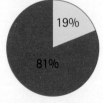

19%

81%

Total value of received humanitarian assistance in $:

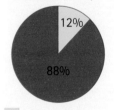

12%

88%

India cyclone (Oct. 15, 1999–Jan. 15, 2000): 91

Mozambique floods (Feb. 1, 2000–May 1, 2000): 382

India cyclone: $40.5 million

Mozambique floods: $290 million

MORE TO THINK ABOUT

The quality of media coverage is as important as the quantity— for example, stereotypes of active white aid workers and passive black victims of famine or disease do not give an accurate picture of the world nor of the reality of poverty.

Q: Can the world's governments bring an end to poverty?

IN SEPTEMBER 2001, all 191 member nations of the United Nations signed the UN Millennium Declaration. This included eight Millennium Development Goals that aim to halve world poverty by 2015. The goals recognize the importance of global partnership between nations if the overall target is to be achieved. Some people have been skeptical as to whether world poverty can be halved, let alone ended altogether!

The leaders of the G8, the world's eight most industrialized countries—Canada, France, Germany, Italy, Japan, Russia, the U.K., and the U.S.—and the president of the European Commission. The G8 meets each year, often to discuss poverty in the developing world. However, the group has been criticized for failing to follow up words with action.

YES

"If the international community is to make poverty history, then there needs to be further coordinated political action by the world's governments . . . aimed at trade justice, dropping the debt, and providing more and better aid."

From text of Early Day Motion proposed in U.K. Parliament

"Yes, world poverty can be a thing of the past if world leaders put their money to it."

Comment in a discussion on the BBC Web site

The United Nations Millennium Development Goals:

1 Eradicate extreme poverty and hunger.
2 Achieve universal primary education.
3 Promote gender equality, and empower women.
4 Reduce child mortality.
5 Improve maternal health.
6 Combat HIV/AIDS, malaria, and other diseases.
7 Ensure environmental sustainability.
8 Develop a global partnership for development.

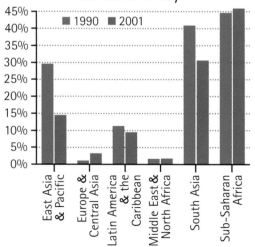

Goal 1—people living on less than one dollar a day

1990 ■ 2001

East Asia & Pacific
Europe & Central Asia
Latin America & the Caribbean
Middle East & North Africa
South Asia
Sub-Saharan Africa

NO

"The end of world poverty . . . exists only in the speeches of politicians and beauty pageant participants. In reality, the world's economy relies on inequalities, and those in power have no incentive to change it."

Comment in a discussion on the BBC Web site

"Since September 2001, the world has too often addressed its problems in terms of conflict, open war, and the rhetoric of militarism, rather than with a commitment to development. This becomes worrisome when considering the prospects for meeting the Millennium Development Goals between now and 2015."

Professor Jeffrey D. Sachs, Director, The Earth Institute at Columbia University, New York

✿ STATISTICALLY SPEAKING

• The World Bank's World Development Indicators 2005 Report found that 400 million people climbed out of extreme poverty between 1981 and 2001. This reduced the world's poorest to 1.1 billion people in 2001—21 percent of the developing world's population.

MORE TO THINK ABOUT

For the poorest countries, many of the Millennium Development Goals must seem out of reach. Yet, if the goals aren't achieved, what will the alternative be?

FIND OUT MORE: www.developmentgoals.org www.oneworld.net
www.globalissues.org

Glossary

Aid assistance, often financial, provided to developing countries by developed countries. Sometimes it is called foreign aid, international aid, or overseas aid.

Artificial wage floor a false limit on wages.

Authoritarian regime a state with unquestioning obedience to the people in charge.

Axis of evil a term first used by U.S. President George W. Bush to describe regimes he believes are a threat to the world order.

Brain drain the loss of skills to a place when the people that possess them move somewhere else.

Budgetary constraints limits on spending plans.

Civil war a war between groups in the same country.

Coercion to force to act or think in a certain way by use of pressure or threats.

Commodity price boom a time when the cost of products is growing quickly.

Conditionality containing certain conditions.

Counterproductive something that obstructs, rather than helps.

Creditors people to whom money is owed.

Cross-pollination exchange of seeds.

Currencies things, such as coins or printed notes, used as a medium of exchange for goods.

Debt money owed.

Debt crisis when a country, usually a developing country, cannot pay its debts to other countries or banks. This term is sometimes used to describe the situation many developing countries are in now.

Degraded reduced in value or function.

Democracy political system in which governments are elected by voters.

Deregulation the reduction of government power over an industry.

Destabilizing upsetting the smooth running of something.

Donors people who contribute something, such as money.

Endowment funds or property that has been given and has the possibility of being a source of income.

Financial institution an organization, such as a bank, whose main activity is dealing in money or financial investments and that does not produce goods or provide nonfinancial services.

Foreign exchange international monetary business between governments or businesses of different countries.

Globalization describes the changes in societies and the world economy resulting from increased trade and cultural exchange. Sometimes, however, it just refers to the effects of trade—particularly free trade.

Group of Eight (G8) – the U.S., Japan, Germany, France, the U.K., Italy, Canada, and Russia. The G8 countries are among the most powerful in the world and meet each year to discuss economic and political policies.

Humanitarian relief assistance given to people in distress.

Implementation carrying something out.

Indigenous originating and living naturally in an area.

Industrialization the development of industry on a large scale.

Inequities injustices.

Infrastructure basic physical and organizational structures.

Interest a charge for a loan, usually a percentage of the amount loaned.

International Monetary Fund (IMF) – an international organization set up to lower trade barriers between countries and to stabilize currency exchange rates. It also offers technical and financial assistance.

Investor an individual or group that commits money in the hope of earning a profit.

Irrigation the supply of dry land with water.

Levy tax.

Material progress having more goods and products available.

Multilateral involving more than two nations or parties.

Nationalization the process of transferring assets from private to public ownership.

Patent a government license giving an individual or organization the right to make, use, or sell an invention.

Privatization the transfer of ownership from government-owned to a privately owned business.

Rhetoric of militarism persuasive language used to suggest that the army and warfare are of great importance.

Rule of law a situation in which government must act according to the laws agreed upon by the society.

Speculation the purchase or sale of foreign currency in the hope that its price will rise or fall, in order to make a profit.

Subsidies sums of money granted from public funds so that the cost of something stays low.

Tariff a duty imposed by a government on imported or exported goods.

Trade/financial liberalization the untaxed flow of goods and services between countries.

Transnational corporation a company that operates in more than one country.

Unilaterally performed or undertaken by only one of two or more parties.

United Nations an international organization with members from most of the nations of the world. It was formed in 1945 to promote peace, security, and economic development.

Utopia an ideally perfect place.

Vantage point a position that gives a broad overall view or perspective.

Veto legal power to overrule a decision that has been made by others.

World Bank one of the world's largest sources of development assistance. The World Bank works in more than 100 developing economies to help the poorest people and the poorest countries.

World Trade Organization (WTO) An organization that controls trade and tariffs between countries to ensure that trade flows as freely as possible.

Debating tips

WHAT IS DEBATING?

A debate is a structured argument. Two teams speak, one at a time, for or against a particular issue. Usually, each person is given a time limit, and any remarks from the opposite side are controlled. The subject of the debate is often already decided, so you may find yourself having to support opinions with which you might not agree. You may also have to argue as part of a team, being careful not to contradict what others on your side have said.

After both sides have had their say and have had a chance to answer the opposition, the audience votes for the team it believes has made the strongest case.

DEBATING SKILLS

1 Know your subject

Research it as much as you can. The debates in this book give opinions as a starting point, but there are Web sites suggested that offer additional information. Use facts and information to support your points.

2 Make notes

Write down key words and phrases on cards. Try not to read a prepared speech. You might end up losing your way.

3 Watch the time

You may be given a set amount of time for your presentation, so stick to it.

4 Practice how you sound

Try to sound natural. Think about:
Speed—Speak clearly and steadily. Try to talk at a pace that is fast enough to sound intelligent and allows you time to say what you want, but slow enough to be understood.
Tone—Varying the tone of your voice will make you sound interesting.
Volume—Speak at a level at which everyone in the room can comfortably hear you. Shouting does not win debates. Variation of volume (particularly speaking more quietly at certain points) can help you to emphasize important points, but the audience must still be able to hear you.
Don't ramble—Short, clear sentences work well and are easier to understand.

GET INVOLVED—NATIONAL DEBATING LEAGUES

National Forensic League
www.nflonline.org

Debating Matters, UK
www.debatingmatters.com

American Forensic Association
www.americanforensics.org

Alberta Debate and Speech Association
www.compusmart.ab.ca/adebate/

index

Acknowledgements

Picture credits: Jeppe Juul/Active Consumers Denmark: 29. © Louise Gubb/Corbis: 37. © Gideon Mendel/Corbis: 40. © Matthieu Paley/Corbis: 35. © Reuters/Corbis: 11, 18. © Kevin Coombs/Reuters/Corbis: 42. Abaca Press/Abaca/Empics: 25. Victor Ruiz Caballero/AP/Empics: 23. Jim Collins/AP/Empics: 32. Antonino D'Urso/AP/Empics: 38. © Paul Fitzgerald, courtesy of *New Internationalist* magazine: 6. Masterfoods Ltd.: 20. © Mark Henley/Panos Pictures: 4-5. © Giacomo Pirozzi/Panos Pictures: 14. Peter De Voecht (SEN)/Rex Features: 30. Reproduced by kind permission of Stamp Out Poverty: 13. Joerg Boethling/Still Pictures: 26. George Mulala/Still Pictures: cover. Hartmut Schwarzbach/Still Pictures: 17. Jorgen Schytte/Still Pictures: 8.

Text credits: Page 6: 1 Frequently Asked Questions About IMF/World Bank, March 2004: http://www.50years.org/factsheets/FAQ-FactSheet_3.9.04.pdf. Page 7: 1 The World Bank: www.worldbank.org; 2 P. Kalonga Stambuli, p. 13, "Causes and Consequences of the 1982 World Debt Crisis?" predoctoral research paper, October 1998; 3 Christie Davies, "Paying One's Debts—Third World Debt Crisis," *National Review Inc.*, 12/17/90. Page 8: 1 address by An Taoiseach, Bertie Ahern, to the plenary session of the World Summit on Sustainable Development in Johannesburg, South Africa, 9/3/02; 2 Dr. Noreena Hertz, *The Debt Threat: How Debt Is Destroying the Developing World*, HarperCollins Publishers, 2005; 3 The 50 Years is Enough Network, "Africa Needs Debt Cancellation, Not More IMF Programs": http://www.50years.org/factsheets/africa.html. Page 9: 1 James D. Wolfensohn, "The HIPC Debt Initiative," The World Bank; 2 World Bank, Debt 2005: http://youthink.worldbank.org/issues/debt/; 3 Vikram Nehru, "Third-World Debt Relief: Indebtedness Just a Symptom of Poverty," *The Atlanta Journal-Constitution*, 6/7/04; 4 Clare Short, quoted in "Debt Relief Will Not Save Africa, Warns Short," *The Guardian*, 1/14/05. Page 10: 1 IMF and International Development Association, "Review of the Strategy Paper (PRSP) Approach: Main Findings," prepared by the staff of the IMF and World Bank, approved by Masood Ahmed and Gobind Nankani, 3/15/02; 2 Simonetta Nardin, "Globalization Activists Debate IMF, World Bank," Reuters.com, 1/29/05; 3 James Wolfensohn, "2004 Annual Meetings Address," 11/3/04. Page 11: 1 Jubilee South, "PRSP Briefing: Poverty Rhetoric & Surreptitious Privatization?" World Development Movement, June 2002: www.wdm.org.uk; 2 Joseph E. Stiglitz, p. 44 and p. 46, *Globalization and its Discontents*, Penguin Books, 2002; 3 Brother Andre, quoted in "Financing Corruption and Repression: The Case of Kenya and the IFIs," Ann Pettifor, 3/12/01: www.jubilee2000uk.org. Page 12: 1 International Chamber of Commerce, "The 'Tobin Tax'—A Business Viewpoint," 12/14/01: http://www.iccwbo.org/home/statements_rules/statements/2001/tobin_tax.asp. 2 U.K. House of Lords Select Committee on Economic Affairs, *Economic Affairs—First Report*, chapter 7, no. 298, 11/18/02. Page 13: 1 U.K. Parliament Early Day Motion, "Cross-party Support for Tobin Tax," Harry Barnes MP, Global Policy Forum, 2/25/02: www.globalpolicy.org; 2 Glyn Ford and Harlem Desir, "Taxing Currency Speculators," *Japan Times*, 11/13/01: http://www.globalpolicy.org/socecon/glotax/currtax/2001/1113tt.htm; 3 Gérard Fuchs, quoted in "French Parliament Adopts Tobin Tax Amendment," Yann Galut, December 2001: www.globalpolicy.org/. Page 14: 1 Oxfam, "Debt and Aid Introduction": www.oxfam.org.uk; 2 Rodrigo de Rato y Figadero, quoted in Box 7, p. 39, overview, Millenium Project Report: http://www.unmillenniumproject.org/documents/overviewEng36-55LowRes.pdf; 3 Helen Hughes, "Third World Aid: Is it Part of the Solution or the Problem?" from *The Australian Financial Review*, 5/11/02. Page 15: 1 Lyn Arnold, "Third World Aid: Is it Part of the Solution or the Problem?" from *The Australian Financial Review*, 5/11/02; 2 Web site "After the Tsunami": http://www.channel4.com/news/microsites/T/tsunami/aid_1.html. Page 16: 1 Oxfam International, "What We Do": www.oxfam.org.uk; 2 Christian Aid, "The Politics of Poverty: Aid in the New Cold War," 2005: http://www.christian-aid.org.uk/indepth/404caweek/index.htm; 3 Clare Short, quoted in "Ethiopia: Is Debt to Blame?" BBC News, 4/14/00: http://news.bbc.co.uk/1/hi/world/africa/713629.stm; 4 Tom Barry, "U.S. Isn't 'Stingy,' It's Strategic," 1/7/05: http://www.irconline.org/content/commentary/2005/0501aid.php; 5 Bryan Johnson, "Changing The Focus of Foreign Aid," 8/25/96: http://www.cdi.org/adm/950/transcript.html. Page 18: 1 Kevin Watkins, "Trade Hypocrisy: The Problem with Robert Zoellick," Open Democracy, 12/12/02: www.opendemocracy.net. 2 President Blaise Compaore, P1, "Cultivating Poverty: The Impact of U.S. Cotton Subsidies on Africa," Oxfam briefing paper: http://www.oxfam.org/eng/pdfs/pp020925_cotton.pdf; 3 Digby Jones, quoted in "Pork Barrel Politics Take a Roasting," *The Guardian*, 5/6/02. Page 19: 1 Neena Moorjani, quoted in "U.S. Appeals Ruling Against Cotton Subsidies," *Washington Times*, 2004; 2 Alan Tonelson, quoted in "U.S. Trade with China: Expectations vs. Reality," Ned Barker: http://www.pbs.org/wgbh/pages/frontline/shows/walmart/china/trade.html; 3 U.S. Import Administration, "An Introduction to U.S. Trade Remedies": http://ia.ita.doc.gov/intro/. Page 20: 1 Institute for Policy Studies, "Why Fair Trade? A Brief Look at Free Trade in the Global Economy," Fair Trade Federation; 2 Equal Exchange, "Fair Trade or Charity Trade?" "Questions...": http://www.equalexchange.co.uk/FAQ.htm; 3 Justino Peck, quoted in "Growers": www.fairtrade.org.uk. Page 21: 1 Gordon Gillet, quoted in "Global Issues Flow Into America's Coffee," Kim Bendheim, *New York Times*, 11/3/02; 2 "Hattie Ajderian: Fair Trade," Posted by Anthony J. Evans on 10/25/04: "Free Trade, Politics": http://thefilter.blogs.com/thefilter/2004/10/hattie_ajderian.html; 3 Felicity Lawrence, "Why I Won't Be Giving My Mother Fairtrade Flowers," *The Guardian* 3/5/05; Page 22: 1 Bangladesh Export Processing Zones, "Prologue": http://www.bdmail.net/bepza/prologue.htm; 2 Simon Hakims and Erwin A. Blackstone, "Description and Evaluation of Free Trade Zones," April 2000: www.temple.edu/prc/ftz.doc; 3 Rose-Marie Avin, "Free Trade Zones and Women in Nicaragua: Exploitation or Empowerment?" From the Spring 2002 issue of WCCN's "Sister State Update"; Page 23: 1 Dan Gallin, Global Labor Institute, Citizens' Agenda 2000, Tampere, "Labor Rights and the Trade Policy of the EU," December 3–5, 1999; 2 edited by Abdul Aziz Choudry, "Effective Strategies In Confronting Transnational Corporations," Asia-Pacific Research Network, 2003: http://www.converge.org.nz/watchdog/04/15.htm; 3 Women's Edge Coalition, from sample findings of case study "The Effects of Trade Liberalization on Jamaica's Poor: An Analysis of Agriculture and Services": 6/10/04: www.womensedge.org. Page 24: 1 Joseph Nye, quoted on p. 110, *The Age of Consent*, Flamingo, 2003; 2 Philippe Legrain, quoted in "Dump Those Prejudices," *The Guardian*, 7/12/01. Page 25: 1 George Monbiot, "A Parliament for the Planet," *New Internationalist*, Jan/Feb 2002; 2 Joseph Stiglitz, p. 21, *Globalization and its Discontents*, Penguin, 2002; 3 Professor Ray Wu, "Stress Relief: Engineering Rice Plants with Sugar-producing Gene Helps Them Tolerate Drought, Salt and Low Temperatures, Cornell Biologists Report," *Cornell News*, 11/25/04; 4 Dr. John Wafula, quoted in "Genetically Modified Crops Are Good for Africa," *Vanguard*, 2/8/05: www.vanguardngr.com; 5 Richard Flavell, quoted in "Dr. Strangelunch," *Reason* magazine, January 2001. Page 27: 1 statement from all of the African delegates (except South Africa) to the UN's Food and Agriculture Organization: http://www.number-10.gov.uk/su/gm_sub2/GaiaFoundation2.pdf; 2 Peter Rosset, "Genetic Engineering of Food Crops for the Third World: An Appropriate Response to Poverty, Hunger, and Lagging Productivity?": www.foodfirst.org; 3 Andrew Simms, summary, "Selling Suicide—Farming, False Promises, and Genetic Engineering in Developing Countries," May 1999: http://www.christianaid.org.uk/indepth/9905suic/suicide1.htm. Page 28: 1 Juan Rivera Tosi, "Andean Wisdom and Consumerism," Issue 1, *Mosaico 21* magazine; 2 Anup Shah, "Effects of Consumerism," 4/18/05: http://www.globalissues.org/TradeRelated/Consumption/Effects.asp; 3 United Nations Environment Program, "Sustainable Consumption: A Global Status Report," September 2002: http://www.uneptie.org/pc/pc/pdfs/Sus_Cons.pdf; 4 Richard D. North, "10 Propositions on Corporations and Consumerism": www.richarddnorth.com; 5 David Dollar, "The Poor Like Globalization," *YaleGlobal*, 6/23/03; 6 International Labor Organization synopsis: http://www.ilo.org/public/english/wcsdg/docs/synope.pdf. Page 30: 1 Sir Bob Geldof, "Controversy as Geldof Declares Himself 'Bored with Africa,'" *Financial Times*, 2/1/05; 2 Bono, "Use Your Collective Clout in Fighting AIDS" 2/24/03: www.u2world.com; 3 Tim Weber, "Davos Touches the MTV Generation," BBC News, 1/30/05: http://news.bbc.co.uk/1/hi/business/4221219.stm. Page 31: 1 Virginia Featherston, "Publicity: The Fame Gain," www.thirdsector.co.uk, 7/17/02; 2 Robert Thompson, "Do Star Campaigners Sway Voters?" CBSNews.com, 10/13/04; 3 Evan Coyne Maloney, "Celebrity Chefs Or, Why I'm Not Boycotting Outspoken Entertainers," 5/6/03: http://brain-terminal.com/posts/2003/05/06/celebrity-chefs. Page 32: 1 Christopher Flavin, State of the World 2005—press release, "Poverty, Disease, Environmental Decline Are True 'Axis Of Evil,'" 1/12/05: http://www.worldwatch.org/press/news/2005/01/12/; 2 Abeja, "Interview with a Terrorist?" 2/2/00: www.worldtrek.org; 3 Kofi Annan, "Today's Threats—Terrorism, Poverty—Require Reformed UN, Collective Action, Says Secretary-General in London Address," United Nations Information Service, 2/10/05: www.unis.unvienna.org; Page 33: 1 Colin Powell, "U.S. Has Moral Obligation To Help Develop Poor Nations: By 2006, U.S. Aid Will Be As Great As Marshall Plan," Global Viewpoint, *New Perspectives Quarterly*, 3/1/04; 2 "George W. Bush: Address to a Joint Session of Congress on Terrorist Attacks," 9/20/01: www.americanrhetoric.com; 3 Walter Laquer, "The Terrorism to Come," www.policyreview.org, August 2004; Page 34: 1 Andrew Simms, "Plunder in Paradise," *The Guardian*, 3/6/02; 2 "Rich Countries Should Pay for Environmental Damage," *Magazine for Development and Cooperation*, January 2005; 3 Jubilee Research "Bringing it All Back Home": www.jubileeplus.org. Page 35:1 Steven Milloy, "Activists, Not Global Warming, a Third-world Threat," Cooler Heads Coalition, 10/22/04: http://www.globalwarming.org/article.php?uid=805. 2 Wangari Maathai, "3rd World Urged to Act on Environment," Water Conserve, 2/8/05: www.waterconserve.info: Page 36: 1 Bill Clinton, quoted on p. 832, "The Curse of Natural Resources," Sachs and Warner, *European Economic Review*, 45, 2001; 2 from interview with Leo Jasareno, chief of the Tenements Division in the Mines and Geosciences Bureau, Manila, Jonathan Glennie, June 2004 in "Breaking Promises, Making Profits: Mining in the Philippines," December 2004: http://www.christianaid.org.uk/indepth/412philippines/Philippines_report.pdf; 3 The World Bank, "Natural Resources to the Knowledge Economy," 2002: www. worldbank.org; Page 37: 1 Catholic Bishops' Conference, "A Statement of Concern on the Mining Act of 1995," 2/28/98: http://www.philsol.nl/A00a/CBCP-mining-feb98.htm; 2 Svetlana Voitiva, p. 41, "Fueling Poverty: Oil, War, and Corruption," Christian Aid, 2003: http://www.christian-aid.org.uk/indepth/0305cawreport/cawreport03.pdf; 3 Michael Ross, "Does Oil Hinder Democracy?" *World Politics*, April 2001, quoted on p. 9, "Fueling Poverty: Oil, War, and Corruption," Christian Aid, 2003: http://www.christian-aid.org.uk/indepth/0305cawreport/cawreport03.pdf. Page 38: 1 BBC Web site comment, 6/19/01: http://news.bbc.co.uk/1/hi/talking_point/1296636.stm: 2 Teresa Hayter, "The New Common Sense," *New Internationalist*, 350, October 2002: Page 39: 1 International Debate Education Association Web site, "Immigration Laws, Relaxation of," 4/24/01: www.debatabase.org; 2 Steven A. Camarota, quoted in, "Immigration, Poverty Linked," Joyce Howard Price, *The Washington Times*, 11/6/05; 3 Text of Howard immigration speech, 4/10/05: http://news.bbc.co.uk/1/hi/uk_politics/vote_2005/frontpage/4430453.stm. Page 40: 1 Gordon Brown, speech to BBC World Service Trust conference, 11/24/05: http://www.bbc.co.uk/worldservice/trust/docs/Towards20050930.pdf; 2 Bill Roedy, "New Initiatives Include Original Nickelodeon TV Campaign and Web Site," 4/12/05: www.millenniumcampaign.org. Page 41: 1 Hans-Henrik Holm, p. 27, "Failing Failed States: Who Forgets The Forgotten?" from "Forgotten Humanitarian Crises: Conference on the Role of the Media, Decision-makers, and Humanitarian Agencies," 10/23/02: www.reliefweb.int; 2 Guy Gough Berger, p. 6, "The Journalism of Poverty and the Poverty of Journalism,": www.sarpn.org.za/documents/d0000311/P262_Berger.pdf; 3 Hans-Henrik Holm, p. 25, "Forgotten Humanitarian Crises: Conference on the Role of the Media, Decision-makers, and Humanitarian Agencies," 10/23/02: www.reliefweb.int. Page 43: 1 from "What Does the 'Make Poverty History' Early Day Motion Say?": www.makepovertyhistory.org; 2 BBC Web site comment, "Can World Poverty End?" April 2005; 3 BBC Web site comment, "Can World Poverty End?" April 2005; 4 Professor Jeffrey D. Sachs, speech at the Bangladesh Economic Association Conference, 6/29/04.